Words of Weight

Mary Grace van der Kroef

Copyright ©2022 by Mary Grace van der Kroef
All Rights Reserved

Cover Art:
"Boulders" ©2022 Mary Grace van der Kroef
Watercolour Painting
All Rights Reserved

Edited by:
Kirsten Pamela McNeill of Worthy Writers Editing

ISBN# 978-1-7777211-3-8 (paperback)

ISBN# 978-1-7777211-2-1 (ebook)

First Edition

Table of Contents

Introduction
Acknowledgements
1. Words of Weight 7
2. Hug 9
3. Be Kind 11
4. Impact 13
5. Forgiveness 15
6. Growth 17
7. Amid 19
8. Understanding 21
9. Spill 23
10. Trust 25
11. Pause 26
12. Grief 27
13. Glimmer 29
14. Truth 31
15. Layers 32
16. Conversation 34
17. Quiet 36
18. Reason 37
19. Punishment 39
20. Resurrection 41

21. Portion 43
22. Sustain 45
23. Virtue 46
24. Guilt 47
25. Worth 49
26. Conscience 51
27. Gratitude 53
28. Conviction 54
29. Compelled 56
30. Bewilder 57
31. Covered 59
32. Doubt 61
33. Persnickety 63
34. Misunderstood 65
35. Progress 67
36. Weeds 68

About the Author

More Books by Mary

Introduction

This collection was written from prompts sent in by my readers at a time when I was feeling low and needed a project to focus on. I sent out a call for words that held meaning for them individually. All thirty-six poems were written from those words, or grew out of those poems as I found words or lines that didn't quite fit, but I still loved. You will find the name of the prompt giver at the end of each poem.

Acknowledgements

Thank you to my readers for your support.

A special thank you to Kirsten my editor
and
Tanya who helped with proof reading.

Words of Weight

Words overwhelm
Some are lead
Others
An enveloping fog

Falling from lips
Hitting the land as boulders
Planting in earth
Rock flowers
Piercing deep
Growing

Some rolling on
Carving
Down to valleys
New waterways

Power from each syllable
Sings
Lightning through the skies
Clouds rain

Pooling phrases
Running wild
Between punctuating
Hedges

Watch the land bloom
Under torrents
Of weighted words
Come drink your fill

Hug

Locked
in the safety
of grounding touch.

Warmth
giving knowledge
of another's life.

Accepted
despite the flow
of wretched tears.

Sharing
life's weight
without a word.

Intimate
trust given
and received.

Released
yet held
in treasured memory.

Lingering
as perfume on skin
despite distance.

(For John)

Be Kind

Ordinary
A lesson we teach to kids
Yet in adulthood
Slighted

Plain concepts
Hard to execute
When wrapped in selfish flesh

Yet infants become heroes
Holding virtues
Boldly
Under pressure

Comforting strangers
Refusing to let the world
Taint their gestures
Of peace

Small acts
Filled with explosive love

Capable
Of slamming shut hell's door

Holy Father
Teach us all
To pour out more

(For Lisa)

Impact

Driving force that leaves a mark
On mind
And body

The slap of thought
That staggers intellect
Forcing reassessment

Yet we walk by
Oblivious
To our impact on others

Leaving invisible ripples
That caress
Or drench

Erosion of barriers
Ours
Theirs
Inevitable

Be it
By crunching impact
That mangles

Or a steady presence
Building connections
As intertwined trees that share
Nourishment
We sculpt each other

Forgiveness

Knowledge
Unerasable, but never sought
Taught
With the back of a hand
Shattered
Character chiselled into a jaw
That never sits straight again

Crooked
Yet set firm in bravery
Unblinking love
Accepting others iniquity
Learning to rise above
Setting free
Self
From bitterness's weight
Others from expectations

Forgiveness
You deceiving strength
Built by a God

Who names Pride a bane
Are there those
Who walk life's path unscathed?
Christ shows his nail scars plain
As He models forgiveness

Growth

Life builds
A living continuation bridge
Curled
Around anchors of moments

Unstoppable
As time pulls us
It's stalks
Across expanses wide
We become walkways
To dance upon

Some warp with the pull
Some splinter
Becoming new entities
Unto themselves
Dropping roots within
Fresh soil

Thin pervasive vines
Or full timbers

We change
Staving off stagnation's rot

(For Jon B)

Amid

Reality spins
Experienced
It threatens to shred

Surrounded
By turmoil
Still held together
Whole
A bafflement of life
To be amid with no control

Listen
To battling choirs
Intoning
Humanity's woes

Still there's purpose
To this sojourn
Separating us from peace
A need that must be filled

Testify
To His promise
As life unfolds
Christ's truth is spilled

(For Andrea S)

Understanding

Be it desired
Is it required?

Can it be comprehended?
Felt beneath the skin?
Sans experience?

Does it demand participation?
Accumulation?
Confrontation of fact?

Left raw
Or baked through life
Can it be digested?

Intellectual
Or emotional
A pinch of both extremes
Lending potency
To empathy

Understanding
Demands humility
While elevated and bold

(For Stephen)

Spill

A mistake
Losing what was meant to keep
A toppling
Horrifying second
That ends as liquid weeps

Different then to pour
A purposeful gift
Flowing from one vessel
To another's lips
A kiss

Something tipped
Falls
Shatters
Who cleans the mess?

Leaving translucent shards
Within a staining puddle
Ingrained
Memory of pain

Thirsty eyes
Left unquenched
Faced with all the waste

Trust

Earned by consistency
Turned by lies
Built on experience's knotted ties

Each knot that's cinched
Another step
A ladder built
Called to climb
This way of reaching the sublime...

If ropes are scaled
Balancing act
Trust that one is holding fast
As life sways
With every move
Anchored

Knowing
Deep in your soul
When one reaches the crest
Both have won

Pause

It pulls
When released in silence
Artful defiance

Burning
With anticipation
Yearning for participation
Vocal
In its separation

I heard it
Pause
An unfilled clause
Awkward in existences
Singing
Its own resistance

...and loved it so

(For Mary)

Grief

Though frozen
By absence
Osteoporosis
Of my soul

Though crumbling
From the inside
Contaminated
By nightshade

Grief is a tool
Of the Master Physician
Friend
Of those in pain

Playing the strings of
Remembering
Sing her bitter lullaby
A cleansing rain

She lingers
Teaching release
Through lessons
Of loneliness

Glimmer

It hints
a luminous sheen.
Helping hidden things
be seen.

It guides
from afar.
Hope of treasures
just past horizon's promise.
But how much?
How far?

Its flirt leaves adventure
open.
Shielding the hidden deep.
Reflecting beams
Secrets to keep.
Still
the world is brighter

for just a glimmer
across the rippling lake.

(For @flourishmom)

Truth

Not perceptions
Not reactions
But what is

Under veils
Under paint
Chipping to reveal

Something feared
Revered
Held at arm's length

Don't look too close
One might choke
Unready to face

It waits
Can't be erased
For what it is

Layers

Layering
The building up of dust
Turf that's warped
Ground
Rough

Soil piling in uneven gallantry
Mountains
Forming valleys as parts of a she

Terrain shifts
Rips with violent quakes
Foretelling of eruption's coming day

A living growing orb
Spewing pressure's liquid rock
Building high ranges
A guard against wind's plot

As the stones are formed
Windward weather rages

Jaded earth is watered
Flourishes in stages

Gradient terraces
Hung above the forest floor
Every pathway climbed
Reveals fresh habitats encore

Climb the crags
Find passes high
Leading on to landwards slopes
Brittle
Bare
Dry

Wander past the grasslands
Sheltering beneath
Hear the whispered love songs
Riding on her breeze

Landscapes ever changing
Built by a liquid core

Created for exploring
While she lays one layer more

(For Mary)

Conversation

Confidence is caramel
Sticks
Drips
Glues
Come the time to speak
And the fight ensues

Process in circles
Outline
Attempt
Reject
Whole sermons spoken in my mind
Answered in kind
As lips fuse with dread

Throw down the logic
Mix well with heart
Watch sculpted reason
Fall apart

Meaningless arguments
A win
A loss
Still
Each a tallied cost

Constant rehearsal
Exhausted
Before the display
Still unprepared
Come the final play
Across wavering tongue

Quiet

I found a moment of solitude in the silence of my heart,
and fell apart.

No noise to hold the fragments of a fracturing mind as one.
Undone by peace.
Given release.

Empty moments,
each playing mystic games with cognitive pieces.

Underneath the mess at rest
something strange reigns.
Breath that blows scattered fragments home.

Regaining self until
prepared again for life's commotion.

Reason

Sanitized steel
Tapered and sharp
Saturated with fact
It slices
Through emotion
Making
Manageable portions

Follow the cut path
Self suspended
Between reality and heart
Permanently paired
By intellect's striking dance
Of understanding

Fact and perception
A battle
Invisible to all but the few
Who look for lines

Around the tired eyes
Of others

(For Jon B)

Punishment

Fear it
A heavy rod to naked back

Avoid it
Always minding well-trodden tracks

Understand it
Dolled out on evil's head

Ignore circumstance
No matter
Scars it will embed

Marking the victim
As one who walked astray

Others recognize
Approved as prey

Self-perpetuating pattern
Conquer, control, conform

Forget correction
Punishment is our norm

Resurrection

Long dead
Dust
Scattered far and wide
Across planes of apathy

Until a glimmer seen
A light that breathes
Seethes
Pushing death aside
Willing dust to rise

Becoming blood
Within veins
Wrapping tissue
Renewing flow
Growing
Muscles breathe

Retrieving
What resignation stole

Resurrecting
Soul

(For Justin)

Portion

Pulled from the whole
Allotted
Set aside for purpose
Direction

Reserved...
It waits for you

A promise of nourishment
Sustaining wealth

Assurance
That you are part of the plan
From His time
You own a portion

Talents in hand
Trusted to flourish

By cultivating
Life

(For Charmaine)

Sustain

As upraised hands tremble
Muscles weaken
Stamina slides
The body cries to continue
What sustains?

Companionship
Through a helping hand
Bearing weight
So another can stand
Lifting higher trembling hands

(For Charmaine)

Virtuous

Existence in opposition
To destruction's plot
A spirit that longs for upright thought
Not perfect
Not a single virtue
But virtuous

Admitting weakness
Still holding firm
An unwavering desire to learn
And give life

Despite the strife
Of daily strain
Amid the monotony of ordinary

Guilt

Afraid to look into the shadows of the edge?
It stands there
Reminding
Confining joy

A tickle at the back of the throat
That no 'ahem' can clear
Soon speech becomes
A jarring dance of sputter
Cough

See it slither closer within the gloom?
Hiding
Waiting
Whispering guilt

Hear it?
I wear it
Smeared lines
Second guessing
How I'm defined

Still there?
Tell me stranger
Has it become me?
Have I become it?

When you look at me
Do you see guilt?

(For Kim)

Worth

What must be done
To obtain?

What must be given
to hold fast?

What balances the scales
Of coins that ask
What is worth?

Man's expectations
Desired accumulations
Nothing else

Yet we ask the question of self…
What is my price?

What would I trade?

We forget
Coins represent time
That can never be bought back

A person is more
Than perspiration's drip

So...
What are we worth?

(For @aletteredlove)

Conscience

It itched
When I took hold
It dragged
When I continued down the road
Giving pause
A redirection of thought
Reminding
Of lessons taught

I could push it aside
Ignore
Convince myself I know enough
To explore
But like a backpack with essentials
Stored
It clings to shoulders
Giving hand holds of
Support

A burden
One shouldn't go without

Regardless
Of human heart's doubt
Let the two
Converse as friends
One asking
One giving plans amends

It acknowledges fears
And dreams alike
Speaking caution
In hushed tones
Silent encouragement
Through a tightened strap's
Groan

Gratitude

A glow that warms the soul
No way to repay this
Kindness

Water
Poured from my own cup
As the one who filled mine
Is remembered

Repeating a truth
That was taught in love
Even when sitting alone

Reminiscing, and missing
Asking, and passing
Acknowledging
A Thank You

Conviction

Thought
With a red-hot core
Upon which shifts
The plates of self

Pressure
Feeds a mind
Stoking molecules
Splitting ideas

Emotion
Spews volcanic truth
Down the landscape
Of understanding

Regenerating
Pummelled opinions
Building high the mountain range
Of Conviction

Guarding
The inner workings
Of a heart set
On existing as a planet

(For Jon B)

Compelled

The road ahead, uneven
Treacherous
The thread that pulls
Is now taut

A compass to the captive
Held in its steady grip
This way, despite stones
Willing feet to slip

Unsure of destination
Holding on to hope
One foot before the other
One thought to contend

Compulsion married belief
Birthed the threads that bind
Compelling man to walk
Take a stand, contract signed

Bewilder

Unexpected trouble
Stops a heart
Within a gasp
Bubbles time
Around a moment
Traps, a grieving rasp

Locks a shudder
With a shiver
Cancelling the lot
Leaving someone speechless
Bewilder
Executes its plot

Know them as an action?
I, a spirit
That's a thief
Robbing words
Stealing time
Stalling breath's release

As an angel
Holds a heartbeat
Steady and true
It's this imp
That makes it skip
Spending bits of you

Covered

Are we covered
For concealing?
Hiding
Forbidden fear?

Or protected
From weather's erosion
Stored
For future use
With gentle care

Were we forgotten
In the cupboard?
A hurried mishap?

Unsettled
Mid our wait?

Or covered
For a purpose

Inheritance
One day He'll claim

(For Estella)

Doubt

A constant question mark
It follows
A shadow overhead

Step on the ripples
At its edge
An attempt to escape

It shifts and drifts
A tether
Attached

Reassuring words dislodge
Giving glimpses
Into the world of light

Only to rebound
On string
Invisible fiend

Cut this doubt
Release
It's lingering twilight

Let it fly on its way
Free
Like I would be

Persnickety

A twitch
Highlights difference
A Shifting gaze
A Nervous tick
Reveals, "I'm uncomfortable"

Upturned nose
Side-sliding glance
A ramrod straight back
Proclaims
I cannot relax.

Make it just so
Even, straight lines
Folded corners, equal amounts
Anything less
And things can't progress

Fussy
Picking
The smallest pilling that reminds

Life wears things down
It can't be stopped

Persnickety humans
They see the details
Are the details
That require
Care

(For @aletteredlove)

Misunderstood

Am I written in hieroglyphics
That you must puzzle
Hypothesize
Mistranslate?

Words spoken
For the wind to cast away

Read my lips
Note my gaze
Every gesture a phrase
Misunderstood

Have you labelled me?
Written your definition
For the word
Forgetting
To listen to the bearer's plea
For time

Fascinated with difference
Convinced of your intellectual prowess
Regardless
Of skipped moments
Avoided interactions
When offered
True connection

Will you be alarmed
When I disappear?

(For Karla)

Progress

Forward
Unstoppable change
Welcomed technology
New ways to engage

With humanity
Nature
The longing to expand
Knowledge that deepens
Humanity's command

Progress
Or progression?
Is there a way to see
If steps bring true
Prosperity?

Or empty change?
Exchanging one slavery
For another

Weeds

Seedlings
Sending up their sprouts
Looking for sunshine
That feeds

Each
A tiny pulse
In nature's map
Until man decides
One is unwanted
A weed

None asked to grow
In this spot
Reserved for his
Endeavours

So few can name
What they pluck

Dandelion
Burdock
Pigweed

Spread
By their Creator
Cast out of
Modern plots
Without thought

Who names weeds?
Humans
Rearranging
God's garden

(For Karla)

About the Author

Mary Grace van der Kroef is a poet, writer, and artist from Ontario, Canada.

She enjoys the simple things in life, like a good cup of coffee and heart-to-heart talks with friends. She uses her writing to highlight those simple things while encouraging others and exploring her own inner world.

She is a follower of Jesus Christ and writes from a Christian worldview.

She believes every person, regardless of circumstance, is a creative being whose stories are important. She cherishes people's differences, and believes diverse stories are imperative to understanding what it is to be human.

Website:

www.marygracewriting.ca

Subscribe to Mary Grace's monthly newsletter by visiting her website and filling out the form on the home page. The newsletter lets you enjoy a monthly update from Mary on her writing and her family life. Subscribing also ensures that you are notified of any special sales on Mary's art or books. Stay in touch and up-to-date by subscribing today!

Twitter: @MGWriting

Instagram: @marygracewriting

Facebook: @marygracewritingRedbubble Art Shop:

www.redbubble.com/people/MaryGWriting/

Shop Mary's various art prints and products on her Redbubble Shop.

More Books by Mary

The Branch That I Am

Praise for THE BRANCH THAT I AM:

"I appreciated the author's insight and identified with much of what she was saying. For those of us who struggle with depression and life at times, Mary Grace shows us that there is hope. I highly recommend this book." - Daniel's Review – Amazon.ca

"Mary's poetic verses are authentic and deeply engaging in their stark simplicity. I felt both uplifted and somehow gratified reading her work as her writing is detailed and visionary in the way she expounds on faith, a prevalent theme in the book. As we wander through life, our thoughts may become heavier, we endure more life experiences that accumulate and change us, and this is an excellent book to read that is very much on par with our inner growth." - Excerpt from Mary-Lisa's Review – Amazon.ca

"I loved how the poems unflinchingly described the emotional agonies of a broken world – as well as how we, in our brokenness, alternatively seek out, avoid, resist, and embrace a transcendent God. The genius of the work lies in it's achingly lovely depiction of the tension between the two: wounded and saved, despairing and redeemed. Highly recommended." - Steve W.'s Review – Amazon.com

Find "THE BRANCH THAT I AM" on Amazon, and other fine online Retailers through Draft2Digital.

www.ingramcontent.com/pod-product-compliance
Lightning Source LLC
Chambersburg PA
CBHW072106110526
44590CB00018B/3332